Praise for *A Thin Band*

"Reading these poems, after the recent death of my husband, grace, and thankfulness, come to mind. Katherin Edwards knows the grief of it. A button dangling from a cuff, blue skies that weep like an elephant, pearly everlasting— these poems are a gentle, timely reminder: to sow our oats and let our gods run wild."
– Susan Musgrave, author of *Origami Dove*

"These poems, like a kaleidoscope, set the world of loss aglow and illuminate the tilt of memory as it tumbles back through years, picks up the pieces, and holds them up as proof of beauty within the fracture of elegy. Unflinching and resolute, yet tender and raw, this collection sings even the names of common weeds into song, and leans hard into the light at sorrow's edge."
– Carla Funk, author of *Gloryland*

"Katherin Edwards' *A Thin Band* is a heartbreaker. The clarity in her lines, the startling leaps in her language, the moral complexity in the imagery itself are nothing short of gorgeous. Though deeply engaged with loss and grief, this is nevertheless poetry about life: how to live in the world, and to go on living, as fully and richly as we can."
– Steven Price, author of *By Gaslight*

A THIN BAND

A THIN BAND

KATHERIN EDWARDS

radiant press

Editor: Kimmy Beach

Book and cover design: Tania Wolk, Third Wolf Studio

Printed and bound in Canada at Friesens, Altona, MB

The publisher gratefully acknowledges the support of Creative Saskatchewan and the Saskatchewan Arts Board.

Library and Archives Canada Cataloguing in Publication

Edwards, Katherin, 1959-, author

A thin band / poems by Katherin Edwards.

ISBN 978-1-77518-397-6 (softcover)

I. Title.

PS8609.D857T45 2018 C811'.6 C2018-905604-5

radiant press

Box 33128 Cathedral PO

Regina, SK S4T 7X2

info@radiantpress.ca

www.radiantpress.ca

For those who were there.

The human heart dares not stay away too
long from that which hurt it most.
There is a return journey to anguish that few
of us are released from making.
– Lillian Smith

FOR THOSE WHO WERE LOVED

FOR THOSE WHO HAVE PASSED

FOR THOSE NOT FORGOTTEN

FOR THOSE WHO WERE LOVED

Waiting for a River

How I hung out my window and waited
like a woman from an Edward Hopper painting,
a lamp glowing warm behind me.
Sometimes, I'd move to the landing
behind the apartment, pretend
I was part of a New York cityscape, smoke
cigarettes, flash ash down the metal steps
uncaring, ready to feign surprise
when you walked through the door. As if
you were coming home and had caught me
unaware. But this wasn't your home, merely
a place to visit, and I'd scurry towards the sound
of your car. Home,
with its glass kitchen cupboards,
great claw foot tub, and gauze curtains
curving in the breeze.
Then there you'd be, swinging open the heavy
Buick door. You'd look up and we'd become a scene.
Roy Orbison singing in the background, *I drove all*
night to get to you. And me, pouring you
a single malt, tying you to me like a ribbon
for the weekend.
And when you'd leave on Sunday,
I'd hang out that window again,
just to listen to your car.
You didn't signal: left, right
but rivered out into the darkness.

Sign Language

Every morning before you left for work
I'd stand at your window waiting
to see the *I love you* dance
as you pulled letters through the air
with your hands
slick as a scarf escaping
a clothesline.
And I heard
for the first time.

Cradle and All

All this falling. We just fell.
And fell each year to greet the fall,
in love with fallen leaves.
Hands held as nights fell, fallen
to our knees, or felt our grace
fall to love.
Out of love, while rain fell
and snow, barometers and stars.
All this falling the one true measure
of all we were and are.

This Is What We Talk about
when we Talk about Blackberries

Blackberries are taking over the yard,
purpling their way up fences, blushing in on the neighbours,
walking clotheslines and peeping into bathroom windows.
They tormented the dog, twirling brambles
around her tail, until she yelped away and never came home.
The berries
become finger paint for three year olds,
rouge for the neighbourhood clown.
Ink for a love letter sent by carrier pigeon.

The stain on the knees of jeans
and hands.
Proof of love.
Tangled, prickly.

February

I vow in this month of hearts
to rage against the love chained
to Hallmark greeting cards.

Today, this first Saturday
of the week before,
I want only to crawl
with a fearless joy
into the marrow of your bones.

List

Passing the junk food aisle of the grocery store,
I find my husband's list and read:
We dance on a thin band of smiles
yet wake each morning with a pack of lies.
I stare at the dented can of beans in my cart.
A two-for-one flyer.
Three fruit flies circling too ripe plums,
and wonder somehow,
if I should shorten
his sentence.

Dinner on Sunday

As you sharpened the knife to cut the roast
you told that joke, and I said,
You slay me,
and left you laughing the loudest
as if that part of our lives was true.
All the while cutting
the rare meat
quivering on the plate.
The knife, squeaking through to the bone.

Discussing the Future

This morning, over oatmeal,
you tied your tie, laced
your shoes, muttering.
I passed you the sugar,
mentioned it was going to snow soon.
This was true. We might have seen the flakes falling
had we stared long enough. I dropped
a plate, rustled the paper, said oh,
look at the time.
At the door, you shrugged
into your overcoat. I noticed
a button dangling from your left cuff.
It was held
by a thread. I leapt
for my sewing kit,
tugged you to the couch,
coaxed the needle up and down.
You watched for snow.
Your hand, dead in my lap.

The Hush

A fly hammers against a window.
The hush moves through the house.
You in one room, me in another. It follows
me into the sewing room,
while you stand at the door,
drink in hand, saying, *I told you so.*
Me saying, *I guess I didn't hear you.*
We talk against walls before silence rolls
like a spool of cotton between us,
a furtive mouse tripping the baseboards.
It's the brown fern in the den.
The dial tone of the phone.
The *click click* of the frozen car Christmas morn,
the unplanted garden in April.
Finally it hangs quiet in the attic,
a noose barely moving.

The House You Walk Into

You could roll a marble
down the slant of this kitchen
or skin a leg on an opening drawer.
You learn to walk uphill
to the bedroom, where your calico cat
mews to be lifted

Tipsy drunk from a house askew,
you learn to rebalance.

Wallpapering Through the Years

More layers than I can count; bold
stripes over deer, lures hooking
fish, rowboats on a canal, perfect
pink roses, a confetti of baby's breath.

Walls grow thick around me, rooms smaller.

Taffeta and tux skim by an open window, honking
cars, a sealed licence.

Rattus rattus

This time, they'll be on the lookout
for the rat. They know how it can collapse
its skeleton, pull the bony body
through a hole the size of a quarter,
go seventeen days without sleep.

This time she'll make sure old love
is contained in an airtight tin;
she'll destroy the lock of his hair,
burn photographs of her past.

He too will be watchful, remembering
how rats chew through concrete,
fray carpets, start electrical fires in bedrooms,
drop twenty feet, escape unscathed.

This time, the two will rub wax
onto the drain pipes, keep
outside lights burning,
seal all cracks, repair
broken glass.

They know.
Rattus rattus is mainly nocturnal;
and too much scratching from inside walls
will drive them both insane.

Unhappy Lover

Did you wish I had drowned in the bath,
from one drink too many and a warmth that was missing.
Did you wish I had given you a chance to pull me from the lukewarm,
happy I was finally quiet. It was the face you loved back then
not how I turned your phrases into singsong
and chanted them back. If I had died, would you have called
my mother, said, not sure what happened, one minute she loved me
the next, she went under.
The shaman at the health food store was right.
He called your eyes secretive,
smooth pools, rain filled. At night
I imagined them spilling over
into our bed, and we'd wake each morning
gasping for air.
So many ways to kill.
Baptism
Submergence
Immersion
Suffocation
Love
So many ways
to drown.

Hate Roars Through

the basement, slashes the heart's
electrical panel, throws switches, cuts
up to the kitchen, illuminates
knives, mallets, bitch
slaps its way past forks,
mixes digitalis with mortar
pestle, measures and doles,
measures and doles,
plots, stalks and drags
its burning body
through dens of lovers,
pawns children, trips
marriages, clutches
from bottomless crevasses,
kills rabbits, sews straightjackets,
spit shines buttons from fossilized
guts of soul, chain polishes
floors, bars doors, bashes
returns, pulls taut on the tethering shackle
of the yelping cur in the backyard.
Panting, twitching,
twitching and panting
hate grooves around
its own steel post
and snarls inward
in a strangling circle.

Old Souls/Déjà vu

There was a chill in the air
the night we sat in your garden.
And as hard as we smoked cigarette
after cigarette we couldn't drag
warmth from our bodies.
Then out of the sky,
mid-July came a soft falling
of thin snowflakes,
and with them, light.

We'd travelled this road
of old souls before
falling out of season.
I'd had visions when we'd last met.
It was in a dusty garden
beside an olive tree. Above us
a window opened,
and a woman called out.
In bones there are no secrets.

Before that moment I saw us in a market,
flash of orange, a scarf maybe, one of us
running. And in the beginning
we posed in a cave
for an artist with red ochre.
Even then, one of us was playing hunter,
the other, lone gatherer.

New Year's Eve

Drink, then search the cupboard
for the twist tie ring a boy gave you in grade three.
Drink to recall the best pet you ever had,
a turtle, whose bones lie
in a soggy matchbox under
a chopped up apple tree.
Drink to recognize the x on the marriage certificate
of your grandmother was a sign of a kiss,
and not a sign she couldn't write.
Drink to smoky days,
a misty river, a mammoth tusk
asleep beneath permafrost.

Blue skies can still weep like an elephant.
Songs from a wren call for the violet cover of night.

Remember, then drink from a brand new glass
raised with a brave hello.

Away

Go to the closet, check the pockets. Forget
the weight of the jacket,
the patches on the elbows,
lint and lost dimes.
I'm telling you, the best days
were not in the office but in the great
thunderstorms racing
across open prairies, sharp lightning
etching the way on a dappled road.
In this country you never signalled
but simply turned. Or not.
Here, was the warped mirror of yesterdays.
What torments you today
will come out in the wash tomorrow.
A west breeze, a full moon, a clothesline
crossing an impossibly blue sky.
Letting go is simply
a matter of unfurling
your hand.

Advice to Self

Drive down the middle of the road.
Stop on green,
wear your wedding ring
on your right hand. Teach your children
to paint the sun black,
the moon purple, collect live flies
and bring them inside to breed.
Walk your father on a leash
and let your god run wild.
Speak in haiku. Put peas up your nose
and sprint with scissors. Don't play
with your food, but dress up your broccoli
and take it out dancing.
Hold doors closed for people.
Live without time.
Prey without guilt.
Step on every sidewalk crack,
break the world's back
one vertebrae at a time
and don't ever be careful.
Go on red.
Just go.

This Time

I'll use invisible thread.
Pull the seams tight,
double-knot the hem if I have to,
gnaw loose strands with my teeth.

If I cut the green stripes
the precise length of the side
(though they won't match the blue)
I know it won't matter.

But the thread is difficult to see.
The fabric won't lie.
Why bother?

I could buy a new dress,
be done with all this mending.
It's not the cost, or the hours of dreary shopping
trying to find something to fit,
it's this dress! It folds well, drapes sweetly
and it's so easy to slip into.

FOR THOSE WHO HAVE PASSED

On Hearing the News of a Friend's Death

In my kitchen, four hundred miles north
I closed the window on the ocean breeze.
The Pekingese hid under the chair.
Mother brought me tea, in a bone china cup.

The Death of Motherhood

The curtain moves with a lonely sigh
a ghost child walks in slippered feet.
Dream from afar, I dream this lie.
She comes to me, a child complete.

A ghost child walks in slippered feet,
her tiny hand upon my cheek,
she comes to me a child complete,
the floorboards shift, the walls creak.

Her tiny hand upon my cheek,
I ache for just one minute more.
The floorboards shift, the walls creak,
she looks back once, slips through the door.

I ache for just one minute more,
as if this dream becomes a truth.
She looks back once, slips through the door,
a child, a dream, my fleeting youth.

As if a dream becomes a truth
I spend my days, stare down the line,
a child a dream, my fleeting youth,
she will be back. I'm almost fine.

I spend my days, stare down the line,
life moves past with a lonely sigh,
she will be back, I'm almost fine,
she was here once, is gone, goodbye.

Walking with Grace

The morning the fire licked through the ceiling
of the old folks' home, the residents were shepherded
to the local funeral parlour. They walked,
strolled and wheeled in a careful parade
past the firemen's hoses, the hurried
water, flashing lights, into the bright
sun, before being directed to enter single file
toward the shadowed foyer.
Not one sad or anxious face among them.
The National wondered why there,
why a funeral parlour?
Surely there could have been a more appropriate spot.
But no, it was the only choice.
The only place big enough,
the only place warm enough,
the only place welcoming, quiet
and close enough.
The only place ready.

Death of Memory

I'm forty-two when the doctor asks
my mother her age
and she says thirty-seven.
When he asks
what floor we are on
and she says tile,
he doesn't grin.
During the math test
counting back from 100
my fingers
work furiously
under his desk.
91, 82, 70 something.
Mother quietly pats my wrist
while she listens
for the countdown.

Her Misnaming of Weeds

Chicory, the sunflower songbird
from Guatemala that sings of sweet longing.

Cocklebur, a small yellow song frog
calling from the hollow of a damp forest.

Oxeye daisy, also known as the pinkeye wink,
is often observed in undernourished children.

Yarrow. The nostalgically-named antidepressant
that works best if taken during brunch.

Common vetch, a trailer-dwelling bat that builds
mud nests under eaves and smells of cantaloupe.

Field Bindweed is the company name of women who possess
outdoor sadomasochistic tendencies.

Chickweeds are girls who keep their pot and don't share. Mouse-ear
chickweed is the soft pouch in which the pot is kept.

Creeping buttercup is when too much butter is placed
in the microwave to melt, and runs out through the cracks of the door.

Teasel is also known as murmuration,
a word for the waltz of starlings
that create patterns while flying collectively
with others.

Death of the Usual

In a field of mustard
there is a shepherd's purse
with three coins.
Wear a bachelor button
in your suit jacket,
sow wild oats and witness
a stork's bill, baby's breath,
your own child born with a cat's ear
and a black cap.
And when the Kentucky bluegrass
is tall in the field, name her Tansy,
him, creeping Charlie.
But beware the black medic
who warns of dogbane at the door.
Fireweed in the bedstraw, scouring rush,
flickering hounds tongue. Flame
in the wee lamb's quarter.
A matchbrush held to the bittersweet
nightshade of this infant, and the green
brittlegrass of morning glory
is gone.
From the Redtop,
all will self-heal over thyme.
Sweet pea, cornflower,
Pearly everlasting, the pennycress
of promise. In the sky,
a yellow starthistle shines on.

The Day His Mother Died

Just left of the office
I hear the man say,
I've ridden bucking broncs and bulls,
but nothing scares me
more than this. Chairs and tables part
as the bed rolls into the death room,
the family follows, the nurse,
pillows for a long night, morphine.
Why is this death different?
Dead horses, stilled bulls, broken backs,
blood and stone. Perhaps it's the
memories swirling like brandy in a warm glass.
How we try to turn the pocket of our heart
inside out, looking for scraps. Or the well-worn
path to the garden.
From the small unzipped
space of body bag
the mouth opens
a final gasp
a last laugh.

Sudden Death of a Child

We didn't recognize the rabid dog until it snapped
at the door with nonstop yipping.
We covered our ears and scrambled to the roof.

My husband threw sticks and I hurled rocks.
It snuck though a window, climbed
the walls, slinked nearer and nearer, till it sat
on our laps, eyes bright, stinking of rag tar.

My grandmother, with blind-eyed war memory,
recalled seeing hundreds of these mongrels stalking the streets.
Smart wives embraced them, fed them fresh cream,
gave them a cold bed, patted their heads with closed fists,
and a weak smile. We dealt, she said. We dealt.

We didn't want to nurture
or encourage it to stay. Still it circled
one way, then the other, until my husband
made a cage and pushed it inside.

Little sister shut herself in the closet and played with her dolly.
Brother shot a hummingbird from the lilac bush.
We made a feather bed
inviting sleep.

We tried for days to tame it but it scratched at our hearts
wanting in, wanting out, playing each of us for attention
till finally we took the tangles from her fur,
bathed, collared, and trotted her tentatively around the block.
Neighbours cooed and stroked, and when we returned

she curled up on the couch, quietly satisfied as if she had always been.
For a silent night, we trimmed her nails,
and when Christmas came we dressed her in red
and walked her to church where we all sang hymns.

Eventually she became furniture we moved about.
Each of us turning to her like a favorite chair.
Placing her on the lawn in the summer, then onto our laps,
her ears turned velvet. In winter,
when her whiskers were light grey,
she left, leaving a cold bed
to sleep in alone.

How the Dead Return to Us

On a beach in Puerto Vallarta,
Bob the dentist sews teeth into sundried fish.
In a dream, my father sits on the ocean floor
ready to pour tea as a sea horse gallops past.
My mother hunches over her walker headed down Main Street.
Same tan shoes. Same green coat. While
my mother-in-law lies on a cot in a cold gymnasium.
She kisses me on the lips. *Thanks for visiting.*
The next day she is dead again.
Thanks for visiting, and it was then I knew.
We visit them. At night
we unhook the veiled curtain
from the thinness of sleep
to fly. Wings beating,
we go when we're ready.

Please Write Soon

Stretched horizontal
on this too soft bed,

this cancer gathers clouds
in a blue moon month.

The mailman walks
past the door again.

Thirteen days
not one word.

To wait means
all time is dying.

Carrier

When we die
and four ounces vanish,
is the lost weight
loose energy, talents
circling our beds, waiting
to land on the quivering withers
of a stray stallion? Does he stand
in a freshly cut field
head turning, hoofs pawing,
ready to carry this gift
down a hard scrabble road?
How else to explain a child's
bruised cheek and scraped wrist.
A fistful of blond mane,
and the ability to play Chopin
before she learns to speak.

When You Are Dead to Me

In my next life I will follow you as
a barefoot castrato
singing arias into the blackened folds
of your vaulted church. A devout son
who rises at three in the light
to change his mother's diapers.
A rancher who strokes the curled
hip bone of a heifer before it's sent
to market. An autistic four-year-old
whose cat purrs as she naps in sunlight.
A woman who sleeps
on Highway One, stopping semis from taking
sad horses to slaughter. You'll know me
as the granite angel in Ross Bay Cemetery.
Wings spread wide, watching
every fall leaf turn red. I will be
two shakes of a die, the reshuffle
of a tarot deck, the last blinking
light in a marquee in Vegas. I will be
the one who makes crop circles smell
like cordite in a wheat field.
I will stand
stone
still.

Stowing Death Away

In the dream of forty days and nights, when the world
was buttoned to the sky, after I'd searched
everywhere, Noah came to me
bearing a gift. In this, he said,
is amnesia. Use it to forget
relatives, friends, erase the colour from your eyes.
Said, who is here, remains.
I watched each pair go forth
clattering two by two,
into a new and lonely world.

The Bitch Known as Nostalgia

is wearing those glasses again,
and clawing the doorframe like a cat
wanting out. It's almost midnight,
and eight days before the moving van
arrives. Before I go, please
unlock these golden handcuffs
of memory. Let's go old friend, round the neighbourhood
swirling champagne in Waterford crystal.
If not there, then the cemetery
like we did after every fall.
I'll bring cheap red, and you'll lay
the biggest leaf at the feet
of the stone angel.
We'll cross arms and burrow,
ask her for another year.
Or, if not there…
Did you know that time runs out
for all of us? Even angels.
Even leaves. Come spring
after a late thaw
you can hold them up to light
and see their cold skeletons.

Mary in Hospice

When I think of her now
I think of the oval
at Stampede Park and the first day
she gave me a leg up
onto a Thoroughbred. Standing
in the shadows, stopwatch in pocket,
she secretly recorded
the quickness of time.

She died quietly.
Bright eyes and polished nails.
A pigeon fluttered on the window ledge.

But it's the Thoroughbred I remember best.
How she ran straight and true
for a goodly mile, how she kicked
her heels as she exited the track.

FOR THOSE
NOT
FORGOTTEN

Neighbourhood Walk

I

The prostitute next door has hung
a collection of condoms
on the line to dry. Working off the old joke
-what did the hooker do
when she was down to her last rubber?
She turned it inside out
and shook the fuck out of it.
But this neighbour checks hers first,
shoves a hose into each, turns on
the water and waits. If they pass the leak
test, up they go. Little rainbows in a row.

II

The Chinese man down the alley
hangs mystery vegetables on his line.
Green leaves in the morning turn
black in the noonday sun.
Seaweed. Maybe. Who's to say?
The next morning, the mystery is gone.

III

Six blocks away a dog howls for its master.
The man died two nights before, and his widow
pinned up his socks. Brown and red,
a few patterned, argyle, golfer's
socks. Six blocks away, a dog howls
for his master.

IV

On the other side of town a man stands
on the stoop, reaches up, pulleys in the empty
line. The squeak opens the neighbourhood
like church bells. Close neighbours
know the man's wife
has left for work, knows he only pretends,
prefers instead to listen to the rumbling
tumble of clothes in the dryer.
Knows the warmth from these towels
is the only warmth he has.

V

On clotheslines a mile away, a quarter section
beyond the horizon, an equator past tomorrow,
someone has hung a placenta,
tobacco leaves, a pair of ears in a box.
Three dollars, scissors,
an entire manuscript like a river
wondering where to begin.

Memory

Memory the fickle bitch wanders the lawn, kicks leaves into a pile, knows pile,
forgets rake, keeps kicking, until she finds a rose, and instead of pressing
the rose into a book, she remembers pressing and irons it flat. Flat
she thinks. Flat she remembers, but not quite taking the long road to flat.
This time there's no time, and Memory wonders if anyone will notice
the slight tinged edge, the faint burnt smell. So she crashes through
the woods, the tangles, the briars, low hanging branches, arrives at flat,
long hall, white lights, and when asked, *how are you today,* she mimics,
fine, says flatly, *today I am fine*. Knows fine. Fine in her world is the rabbit
of the gamekeeper. A fine catch, a sleek coat finely turned out. A fine head
and velvet ears flopped over the gamekeeper's fine shoulder.
So alive one minute, so limp the next.
So fine when quiet.

Christmas Card

It's unclear who quit sending first; when
the last Christmas card with the picture
of a snuggled-in cabin arrived, its tilted
chimney puffing out smoke.
The worn path to the door. You can just imagine
the fire inside, the stories told, like the enclosed letters,
tales of first born children, marriages, travel and grandkids,
sickness and pain, until we both became less
news, no longer lit by the north star.
On the card not sent there is no path to the door,
there is no door, only snow falling.

What I Saw in the Forest Today

A fire pit with a melted bottle at its core.
A tree still standing, its neck laced with axe marks,
sap joining the cuts. Four legs of a small deer stacked
like firewood. Tiny hooves pointing the directions of a compass.
And stops signs.
Large, red signs.
Warning motorcyclists to stop, stop
before exiting the veined trails, before
crossing the main road.

What I saw in town today:
A coyote running
toward the local coffee shop
on main street,
straight as an arrow
looking for home.

Family Plot

A graveyard tilts
against a hill
where my brother lies
chewed through a combine.
Next to him, a plot for our father
exhausted from cigarettes.
A grandmother I never knew
moss blinding her death date, holes
from granddad's walker
circling, circling.
And locked deep
beneath fresh dug earth,
you, my love, spilled
from a red tractor.

Frost hangs
across half-ploughed fields.

Birds sing.
Days ache thin.

Clear Skies

There were never birds
in the city centre
save the odd screeling
lost gull.

We lived bright
but there were
no birds.

Prayer for a Prairie Town

God return me to the slumber
of homesteads, glass doors,
leaded windows.
Give me a day
fresh with breezes
sheets snapping on a clothesline
sweet picnics and lemonade.
Kitchens where chickadees flit
past lace curtains, where roads
sing from early spring rains.

And deliver me oh Lord, from failing
dark churches, broken glass
one-eyed trucks
rusty tricycles
and grant me

one fine sunflower
a house to repair
a box of nails.

In Sickness

Half way we stall,
climb out,
kick the tires
push her to the top
where we believe,
if we shove hard enough
she may coast, re-fire.

A passing couple suggests
the timing may be off,
can't hear no rhythm,
others wonder
about the direction,
the projection,
why we were headed
to the highway's cross.
That particular dirt road.
To be here now.

And as we wait for help
at the gravel stop,
stones are tumbled
balls volleyed, coffee drunk,
tinkering occurs, naps are taken.

Finally the mechanic arrives
shakes her head
sighs, and everyone waves
goodbye.

Post autopsy, the bright key lost,
I'm forced to think new,
think work, think
get creative, think
hard solution, think
follow anything.

The breeze shifts.
Down the road
a lone cur skulks
through a box canyon.
A cow stands on a hill.
I retie my boots.

After Harvest

My father mute,
cancer blackening his lungs

nothing to be done
the surgery a sham.

Quiet as a scarecrow
sun on his back, autumn smoke
drifts lazy in the sky
the creek trickles to dry

Barn swallows conduct
fields with the grace of autumn.

Sleeping Dogs

Wake them, make them tell the truth
and they'll tell you about
circling blocks at the end of a leash,
twice daily, in the same direction, past a hydrant
at the corner of 6th and Main, a calico cat
on the hood of a truck, a stand of dead
poppies in an abandoned parking lot.
But in their dreams
they have travelled miles.
Pulled children
from wells, posed in tapestries
and tombs, treed cougars
and outrun gazelles in Africa.
In dreams,
we all
lie well.

Midway Meditation

Pay six tokens for fear,
pocket a prayer, hang like a spider,
fly from swings without wings,
tilt the world for three minutes or less.

Live this moment between breaths
don't imagine shopping lists to be crucial.
Forget to go home and water the raspberries.
Here is here and now.
Not to say that flying is living
and stillness is not,
but to say, for a moment
we feel what birds live.
Hollow bones, space-filled minds
elegant flight.

Light

It's a minute after midnight.
Tip the bottle a little this way friend.
There may be a drop at the bottom.

Acknowledgements

Thanks to the editors of each of the following publications in which some of these poems appeared in earlier form:

Arc Poetry Magazine
The Malahat Review
The New Quarterly
This Side of West

Thank you as well to Jack Pine Press as some of the poems were published in *The Sky Was 1950 Blue.*

Huge love and thanks to Donna Kane for always being my first reader, and for always being kind. And for Cliff. Always for Cliff.

Special thanks to Steven Price, Carla Funk, Lorna Crozier, and Susan Musgrave: instructors extraordinaire. And Sean Virgo, friend extraordinaire.

Gratitude to Kimmy Beach for her bravery in editing this work, her light touch, and wicked humour, but especially for tying this book together, and to Debra Bell and Radiant Press for taking a chance.

Katherin Edwards

Katherin Edwards has her MFA in writing from the University of British Columbia. Her fiction has appeared in the Malahat Review as well as the collaborative novel At The Edge. Her creative non-fiction has appeared in In This Together. A two-time winner at Eden Mills for poetry, she has also been published in Arc, The New Quarterly, as well in chapbook form with JackPine Press.